The Lord's Prayer In Japanese

Colouring Book

The Beautiful, Simple to Colour Characters
of the Japanese Language

主の祈り

ぬりえ本

MAGDALENE PRESS

The Lord's Prayer in Japanese Colouring Book
The Beautiful, Simple to Colour Characters of the Japanese Language
by Esther Pincini

主の祈り
ぬりえ本

Copyright © Magdalene Press 2018

ISBN 978-1-77335-112-4

No part of this publication may be reproduced, stored in a retrieval system,
or transmitted in any form or by any means, electronic, mechanical, photocopying,
recording or otherwise without written permission of the publisher.

Magdalene Press, 2018

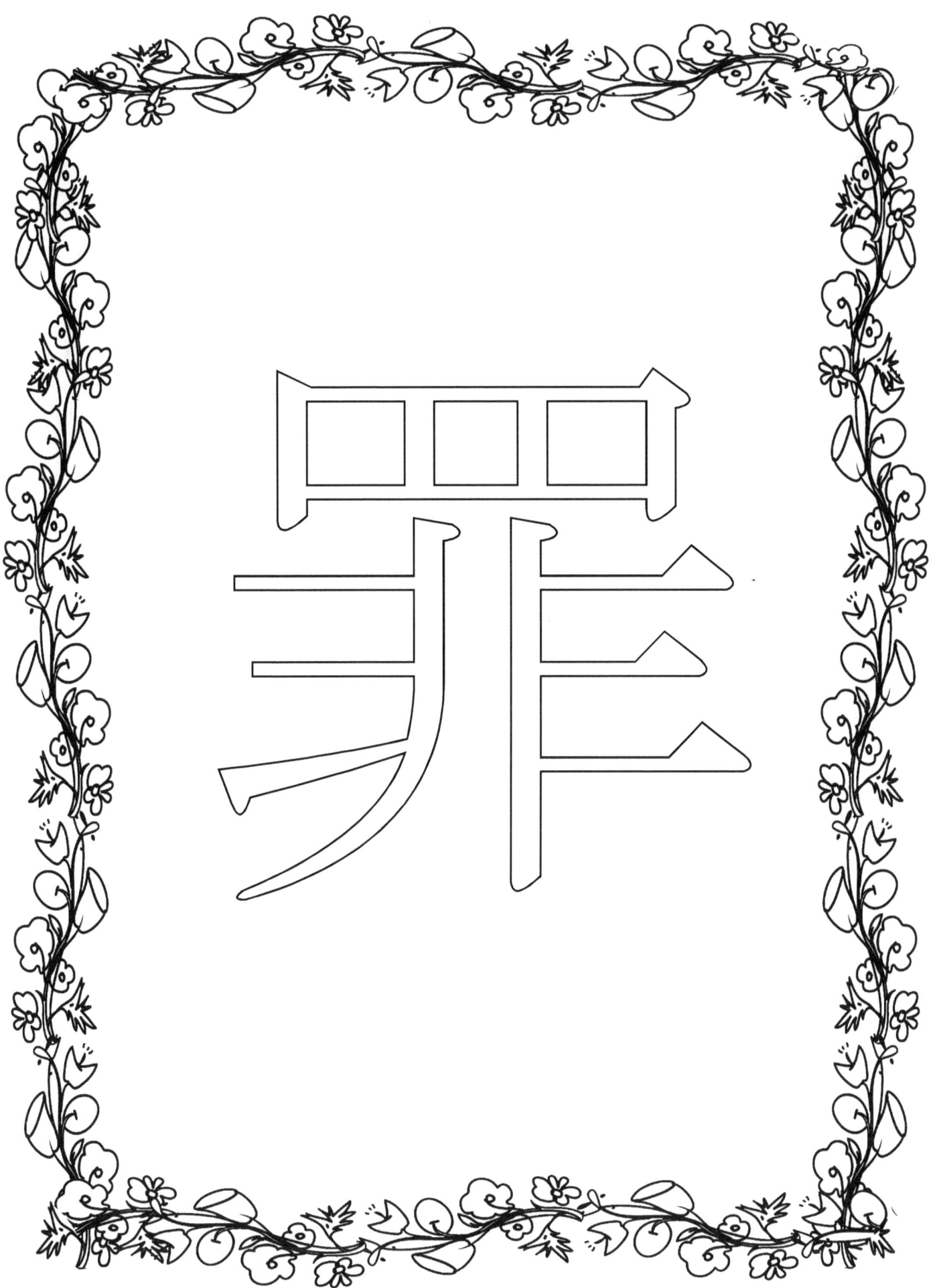

Japanese / Transliteration / Translation

天におられる私たちの父よ
Ten ni orareru watashi-tachi no Chichi yo
Our Father in Heaven

み名が聖とされますように
Minna ga sei to saremasu yo ni
Hallowed be Thy name

み国がきますように
Mi kuni ga kimasu yo ni
Thy kingdom come

みこころが天に行われるとおり
Mi kokoro ga ten ni okona wareru tori
Thy will be done

地にも行われますように
chi ni mo okonawaremasu yo ni
On earth as in heaven

私たちの日ごとの糧を今日もお与えください
Watashitachi no hi goto no kate o kyo mo oatae kudasai
Give us this day our daily bread

私たちの罪をおゆるしください
Watashitachi no tsumi o yurushi kudasai
And forgive us as we can forgive those who sin against us

私たちも人をゆるします
Watashitachi mo hito o yurushimasu
And lead us not into temptation but But deliver us from evil

私たちを誘惑におちいらせず、悪からお救いください
Watashitachi o yuwaku ni ochi irasezu, aku kara o sukui kudasai
For Thine is the kingdom and the power and the glory forever

アーメン
Amen

www.ingramcontent.com/pod-product-compliance
Lightning Source LLC
Chambersburg PA
CBHW051120110526
44589CB00026B/2984